Praise for *Silent Screams*

"Gutsy new writing."
– Gail Johnson, Health Editor at *The Georgia Straight*

"Every piece is written with genuine expression, threaded together with a golden needle. The poems eloquently describe the unrelenting injustice of an eating disorder and the glorious magnificence of recovery. If you have ever wondered what it's really like, prepare yourself for this profound, courageous journey of one who has saved her own life."
– Shelley Jensen, CPC, eating disorder therapist

"The poems provide valuable insights into the emotional journey one takes on the road to recovery."
– Christine A. Hartline, M.A., Director of the Eating Disorder Referral and Information Centre

Other Books by Lori Henry

Dancing Through History: In Search of the Stories that Define Canada

Silent Screams

Silent Screams
Into and Out Of Bulimia Through Poetry

Lori Henry

Dancing Spirit
Publishing

Vancouver, Canada

2014 Dancing Traveller Publishing paperback edition
Dancing Traveller Publishing, Vancouver

All rights reserved. No part of this book may be reproduced, stored in a retrieval system, or transmitted, in any form or by any means, without prior written permission of the publisher, except in the case of brief quotations embodied in reviews and articles. In Canada, in the case of photocopying or other reprographic copying, a licence can be obtained from Access Copyright (Canadian Copyright Licensing Agency): www.AccessCopyright.ca.

Request for permission to reprint anything in this book must be made in writing to the author: lori@eatingdisordertherapist.ca.

© Copyright 2014 Lori Henry
www.eatingdisordertherapist.ca

LIBRARY AND ARCHIVES CANADA CATALOGUING IN PUBLICATION
Henry, Lori, 1982-, author
     Silent screams : into and out of bulimia through poetry / Lori Henry. -- Third edition.

Originally published: Victoria, B.C. : Trafford, 2002.
Issued in print and electronic formats.
ISBN 978-1-4357-1843-2 (pbk.).--ISBN 978-0-9876897-2-6 (html)

1. Bulimia--Poetry. 2. Eating disorders--Poetry. I. Title.
PS8565.E594S5 2014 C813'.6 C2014-907685-1
                              C2014-907686-X

For those whose lives have been affected
by an eating disorder.
Although your resiliency is being tested,
know that your courage is strengthening.

Preface

This collection of poems was written during my battle with bulimia. Starting at 12 years old, I began a dangerous dance with an eating disorder that would take over my life for the next six years, and many more during my recovery. I was able to hide my behaviour better than anything else in my life and became the best liar I have ever known (until I met others who were also struggling and were just as deceitful as I was).

I took my first dance class when I was two years old and performed on stage only one lesson later. I fell in love with the exhilaration that performing brought and quickly got used to the fast-paced lifestyle that future dance classes demanded. I tried new disciplines shortly after and was soon in the studio almost every day of the week. My life became a whirlwind of activity as I tried to balance school, dance, sports, friends and my social life. The busier I became, the more I stifled my feelings until I had become completely numb. My relationship with food followed suit and I developed a strict regime that I thought would simplify it all: dieting. Obsessing over calories and an exercise regime funnelled the complications in my life into one simple formula: restrict my food intake and exercise excessively.

Instead of happiness, though, I was constantly fixated on numbers, dividing food and behaviour into "good" or "bad," and driving my perfectionist attitude to a fanatical extreme. Everyday was a battlefield within myself to try and lose weight faster. I was convinced that my teenage worries were trivial compared to the much more "important" goal of being skinny.

Yet as the behaviour intensified, the toll on my body and mind throughout those years eventually became too great and I broke down one day from sheer exhaustion. I walked into my school counsellor's office and could not stop the tears that gushed from my fragile body. Thus began my journey through recovery, relapses and eventual healing.

The years that followed were filled with doctors, therapists, nutritionists and councillors, all trying to shift my distorted beliefs into a more balanced state of mind. It took me many years to sort out the damage I had done to myself mentally, physically and spiritually. With my mind bent on self-destruction, health initially seemed like an impossible task.

After a trip to Paris when I was 19 years old, I realized that writing was the only thing that had kept me afloat during the countless times I wanted to give up. I began looking through all of the journals I had kept from grade six onwards and found some really powerful, if not rough, poetry. I decided to edit the poems into a full-length book, more for my own recovery than anything else. It turned into the first edition of *Silent Screams*, published in 2002.

The book was an amalgamation of all the things I could not say while bulimia had its grip on me. In time, I discovered that this writing could also help others who were caught in their own disordered eating web. I began doing talks in high schools, for youth groups, at seminars and at a dance convention about my experience. I found out how many people could not only relate to what I had been through, but knew someone who had suffered or was suffering from an eating disorder.

This work led me to publishing a magazine called *Beauty: You Define It*, which was distributed into high schools and encouraged teenagers to define beauty in their own terms. It examined the media's influence, body image and culture through articles, poetry and artwork. (It was not long afterwards that Dove launched its well-known "Campaign for Real Beauty.")

I then found myself writing again, this time a column dedicated to eating disorders where I could educate, field questions and offer resources for people seeking up-to-date information. I was also battling the entertainment industry as I pursued my acting career in a business where looks meant everything. In order to have the flexibility to work in the film industry, I took on freelance writing jobs to supplement my income. Before long I was doing more writing than acting and amassing quite an extensive portfolio.

After returning from France on a trip to Provence in 2006, I submitted a travel story about Avignon to the Vancouver Sun. It was accepted. The publication of that article introduced me to the enticing world of writing about travel. I immediately began penning tales from recent trips I had taken, marrying my passion for travel with my love of writing. I would go on to become a travel writer full time, jetting off to countries like Japan, New Zealand, Jordan, Romania, United Arab Emirates and Thailand on assignment. I was treated to a 12-course meal in Kyoto, opulent cuisine in Dubai, and gourmet vegetarian and gluten-free menus at the Grail Springs wellness centre, pausing every once in awhile to reflect on a time when I could not have imagined being around such copious amounts of food and not binging and purging to relieve the anxiety. Yet there I was enjoying myself with new friends in intriguing cultures, focused on finding interesting stories to tell, not worried about where I would purge after the meal.

This must sound impossible for those who are going through a battle with an eating disorder but my recovery began small: I started by expressing the things I kept hidden from everyone else and putting them into words. That release enabled me, along with therapy, to begin dealing with the issues beneath my obsession with food and weight. It is possible to get to a place where food doesn't hold the power to control your life. Start now. Here. With these poems.

This collection of poetry highlights the pain and fear that used to rule my life and is mostly addressed to the eating disorder itself. I have decided to make only a few minor adjustments to the poems as they were written so many years ago. They may not be elegant but they are true to the pain I was experiencing.

May no one's screams go unheard.

Lori Henry
Vancouver, 2014

She
(Part one)

As day conspires into night
and the household retires to sleep,
she is left in complete and utter silence.

The journey within reveals
her tortured soul as it awaits its nourishment,
hungrily anxious to devour
the constraint it exercised throughout the day.

The night's stillness opens doors
into the unexpected,
the dark corners of a young girl's mind
as she lies in bed, half asleep,
listening to the voices that have taken
her mind hostage:
they direct her to follow them,
a melody so sweet she cannot resist
the comfort they chant in her ear.

She creeps down the staircase
lost in a fog of swirling conflict,
fighting the voices who will not allow her

to awaken pure.
But the voices shift into distorted sounds,
images of daunting T.V. shows, horror films,
repeating themselves like
a maniacally skipping CD.
The natural impulse to feed her starving body
has turned into a nightmare of
unyielding cravings again tonight.

Descending onto the final stair
she can almost smell the sweet aroma of fulfillment.
The kitchen draws nearer
and the images more vivid –
the only thought that enters her mind
is the need to consume.

In the darkness of night
the freezer opens,
then the fridge;
the microwave hums to life.
Her taste buds are already savouring the flavours
before they slide down her throat
into her ailing body.

But wait –

she hears a door,

then footsteps.

She is sure of her intruder

and the threat of being caught –

blind terror paralyses her limbs,

stopping time in its tracks.

The noises cease.

All she hears is the beating of her own heart

and the quickness of her breath.

Back to the task at hand.

Filling her soul with the rich substance

of fulfilled desire,

the feeling of not being lonely anymore;

all of her needs subside

except for the simple action of hand to mouth;

the guilt that festers inside of her

burns deeper than she will ever show.

But back there she will go,

night after night,

craving something to ease her hollow pain.

The tension rises in her gut
as she realizes what she has done;
all of her hopes and dreams vanish
with the thought of gaining weight.
Violent panic seizes her tired body –
there is no other choice,
she must get rid of it.
Like a wild animal
fighting for freedom
she fiercely purges what she cannot say.

Then the moment of stillness,
calm,
relief.

But the mess lingers in her consciousness,
leaving behind an irremovable stain.
Not only does she have a full kitchen to clean
but her emotional secrets are scattered
across the room:
walls,
the ceiling
and the floor all bear her shame.
Such a mess to clean up.

But the incessant voices

are not there to help her now;

their job is done for the night,

leaving her there, helpless,

to pick up her shattered self alone.

The sun shines through her curtains

as she hears the clatter downstairs –

no one is the slightest bit aware

of her destruction the night before.

How can they not notice such a nauseating mess,

a mess never really cleaned up?

It still lies scattered around,

left to be covered up and buried

with the rest of the morning's feelings.

The day carries on.

She is good today,

only eating the "right" foods,

receiving compliments on her discipline,

willpower,

restraint –

it seems that is what she needs

to keep herself on track.

But as the sun draws its last ray of warmth,

the girl finds herself back

where she was the night before,

helpless to a ruthless power

too overwhelming to overcome.

Tumult

Terror

of myself

runs deeper than my soul,

harder than my pride,

vaster than my ego –

stuffing it down,

wrenching it up,

grasping for dear life

and running like hell.

Lost

This horrible stench

corrupts my freedom

and helps me run from the truth –

reality bleak

as I sit on this stone

and count my wishes again.

And again.

Wanting

I want to go

where the day will take me,

swept away by night

and caressed in the morning;

a foreign landscape

of flashing lights

beckons me nearer,

fever burning

into my skin

until I cannot help but fly.

New tides rush over my body

and lift me onto the waves

where I sail up high,

feel the air

and expand my withered wings.

Useless Tears

I weep my lonely tears
as I tremble on the floor;
I hate to see myself like this
when the pain is so unbearable –
from nowhere and everywhere at once –
I want to dull it,
but I need sleep so desperately.

I keep trying to repair myself
without a chance to just *be* –
I cannot imagine the freedom
of unselfconscious steps,
yet I do remember fleeting moments
when I let the wind blow hair from my face.

My freedom hides where I cannot listen –
or maybe I choose to be deaf.
I cannot hear the tune of my own song
as it is drowned by the noises of others.
So I stay quiet.
I prefer the solitude.

Hope

I exist,

so do you;

the difference is

I do not live inside my body.

I despise it.

We are like the vilest of enemies

who work against one another,

testing who will destroy the other first.

I sometimes look at myself in the mirror

and wonder how it happened –

when was it I started detesting myself,

what makes me do it,

and can I stop?

I hope one day I will be able to

embrace myself truly, honestly,

forever.

Vilest Self

I hate being me –
all that surrounds me means nothing.
Take back the perfection,
what do you get?
An empty vessel
with a smile.

Leave me alone
to explore my darkest realm.
I will be fine if you just leave me alone.

A Little Deeper

I am in the depths of my chamber
grasping onto life,
clutching my heart as it threatens to burst –
look at me now.

Not thinking straight,
mind in a daze,
somebody take my tortured soul
and rip it out,
who needs it anyways?
Give me anything tarnished –
bleed me, punish me,
torture me to death.

I cannot believe how much I hate myself.

My Friends

Where are all my friends –
did you disappear while I blinked
or has it been ages since I last made contact?

I am lost
in a world with no one around me
but blank faces staring,
judging and questioning –
I cannot find my way home.
I have pushed you away
and locked the door,
leaving myself lonely
and confined –
yet I hopelessly wait for your knock.

The Road Less Dangerous

I feel I have travelled this road before
one too many times
and I do not like the scenery;
the same old bends
the same old curves
greet me at every corner.

This road has a low speed limit
but my car will not delay,
yet as it speeds along
I seem to be going in reverse.

Do not tell me again
that I cannot get off,
that this is the only way to go –
I do not believe you.
Because the road to my right
and the road to my left
both look less dangerous to me.

Vancouver Rain

I look outside to the downpour of heavy rain,

but instead of being

buried under its weight,

I see how each beautiful crystal of moisture

shimmers in the limited light;

I am comforted by the sound

of raindrops dancing on nature

and I now love the rain

for soothing my anxious soul.

Replaceable

The porcelain doll cracks
and everyone cries –
what will happen now?
The poor thing.

Shall we throw her out
or should we keep her?
No, we will just replace her
with another beautiful doll.

Easy To Feel Pain

I look into my own eyes
and see the immense pain –
where did it come from?
If it came so easily
to imbed itself into my pores,
why won't it leave
the same way it came?

Save Me

Engulf me, rain,
wash me away
into oblivion;
sweep me past the day-old trash
into the gutters of my mind.

Engulf me,
save me from the voice
that compels me to destruct,
and drown its hideous sound.

A Place To Put It All

Softly I open my eyes
to blink at the darkness,
eyelashes gently
brushing against my sullen cheeks –
tears flow endlessly from my heart,
lake upon ocean,
as I feel the same raw pain
again and again.

Those little things that shake me
and rock me from my boat
carry me off into a foggy haze of doubt,
where all transpires to my waiting pen.

Avoiding Myself

Just push them away.
All the pain,
all the memories,
all the scattered tears –
maybe they will leave me alone
if I just push them away.

Sunless Void

I am sitting here in my heart of darkness.
I feel so small compared
to the heavy black fog surrounding me;
it is the ugliest void I could ever create,
yet it is me.
As I sit within it,
calmly and serenely,
the darkness does not lift
but the light seeps in;
and it does not seem
so hideous anymore
and it does not look
so loathsome.
It is my heart.
It is my soul.
It is me.
And I will not be ashamed.

Barren Self

I am empty
yet I look full,
and no matter how much
I stuff into my body
I realize just how depleted I am.

Take away the fat,
can you see through me?
Like a hollow Barbie I weep,
draining all I have left
onto my painted face.
I am empty.

Muffled Cries

I am defeated,
sold my soul to society;
let it crush down on me,
let me get in the way,
exhausted and abused
I will make myself pay.

And then I am silent,
having used up my fear,
as I lie on my carpet
praying no one will find me.

I lift my head
and feebly cry out,
but no one comes running
in this big empty house;
no one will save me
in this big empty house.

Waiting

Rivers of tears flood down my cheeks,
glistening in the light;
sparkling tears running freely
from a weeping child's fears.

So beautiful they caress
each curve and each crease,
longing for a place to settle –
with each new drop of dewy liquid
another comes tumbling down;
a parade of beauty
waiting to see the light,
waiting to be let out
from the darkness they were born;
waiting to be free
to fall wherever they may
and magically release my fear.

Freedom

You have reached that longed for place –
how did it come so easily
and why did it choose you?

I have been trying to catch it
for so long now
and when I see the glow in your eyes
I know that you have found it.

But I can barely smile
because I want what you have found
and you suit it so nicely;
my happiness for you is cautious –
will there be any left for me?

Tell Me Something

Tell me that I am worth it
good enough to love;
tell me not to worry
I am fine the way I am;
tell me that you love me
through your honest eyes;
just please tell me something
to disprove these murderous lies.

Hold Me

Sometimes I feel like giving up
when fighting seems in vain,
energy drains from my shrinking self
and I need somebody.

Sometimes I feel like falling apart
when rage consumes my body,
I want to scream and shout and hate you more
but accept your dark fate.
Hold me tightly in your arms,
hold together my breaking soul
that shatters underneath.

Sometimes I feel like hiding away
when I am touched too much inside,
quietly quivering alone in the corner
without anybody.

Sometimes I feel like killing my demons
when I am strong enough within,
I want to fight, I will win
but I still need somebody.

Sometimes I feel like achieving my best
when my heart is light and free,
nothing will stop me or get in my way
and I take up space with pride.

Sometimes I feel whole and complete
when each breath fulfills the next,
I am independent and wildly free
but I still need somebody.

All I Need Is A Break

I am sick of fighting it,
so exhausted from trying
and failing –
where is my motivation?
I am just a skeleton inside this body
and will break if you push me.

It seems as though you have won;
I cannot find the strength
to confront you right now;
you deserve an execution
but I cannot pull the switch.
Just let me be
for one day,
until I am strong enough to take you on –
all I need is one day free of struggle
and I can start the fight again.

No More Pleasure

I am wasted,
purged of sin,
fear and guilt –
so why has nothing changed?
My throat a desert,
my limbs hollow,
I feel heavy yet breakable –
I gave it all up
to feel this way,
but what have I received in return?

Guilt lies heavily on me now
like a winter's coat,
draped over my shivering soul.

Beneath My Calm Exterior

I hate it when you creep into my thoughts
to disappoint and anger me;
I have been let down and walked upon
by your selfish boots
for too long.
All the nasty tricks,
the bullshit lies,
the fictitious support you have given me –
no more stomping on my soul
and laughing.
I lash out with my fists,
thrash with my arms,
while calmly carrying on.

The Mindless

I sit in a stall

with my desk and computer

watching the minutes waste by –

all around I hear bullshit and lies

I am told to say

with a smile;

but smiles are what I hate the most

when surrounded by talking machines,

who argue and aggravate

the random selections

with laughter and twirls of their seat.

Comfort In This Grave

You are my angel.

Your sweet breath forms the words

I long to hear,

your sweet smile

brightens up my dark day,

your sweet touch

reminds me I am touchable,

your sweet voice

tells me you love me,

unconditionally,

and that is what I need.

I will never forget.

My Fault

I feel so guilty
and I cannot move on –
it feels as though a heavy brick
was dropped into my stomach.

I hate feeling like this
and I hate that
I have done it to myself;
no one around,
just me and my obsession –
all I do is abuse myself
and then cry.

I am so sick of dealing with it
and what it puts me through,
but I just cannot stand up and fight;
my strength has been forced out
and I am left powerless.

Consumed

Torment,

utter anguish

piercing through my soul

taking,

always taking away

what is left of my beauty –

I am left in a heap

of myself on the floor,

too consumed to even moan for help.

Give Me, Leave Me

I want you. I need you.
You despise me.
As much as I hate you
do not ever leave me,
comfort me through everything,
please;
you destroy my spirit
and tear me apart,
yet soothe my soul
and satisfy the gnawing cravings,
for awhile.
I hate you.
You ruin my willpower,
my body,
my life;
you take away my confidence
and layer me with fat,
you cover everything up
and pretend it is okay.
I trusted you.

Now just leave me alone.

It

Destruction of all I create
hinders my sleep –
my anxiety deepens
as this nightmare unfolds –
my body is overflowing with trash,
my soul is submerged with demons,
my head is filled with you.
And you.
And you.

Breaking The Cocoon

Fresh face

vibrant smile

eyes open to face the world;

body alert

and ready to move

in ways of only a dream.

I am ready to fly.

Wasted Efforts

I am all out of hope,
used up and wasted
and ready to leave;
maybe I will do better next time around.
I have scattered parts of myself
all over this town
and now I am left empty and longing.
I want something, anything
to satisfy this gnawing
deep within my stomach,
but I am grasping at nothing
and receiving nothing in return;
I am in so much pain
that I tremble inside
until I fear I will explode,
but it never quite happens.
I have torn apart my soul,
leaving it scattered;
I have raped myself
of everything I ever had
and it has not done a damn thing
but cause me more agony.

Strength I Cannot Find

This sinking feeling in my heart hurts,
physically hurts –
I am pained to think of my imperfections.

My candlelight flickers to darkness
and I am back at the beginning;
although my soul has grown
and my heart beats stronger,
I still find myself
battling too many sleepless nights,
brain and tears working overtime.
I hate this,
yet I cry instead of fight.

OK State of Mind

Go to bed, my tired soul,
nod off the evil day
and calmly let morning come.

I am in an OK state of mind
ready to fall asleep;
there is no need to worry tonight
because I will make it 'til tomorrow.

Put away the wet Kleenex
and soothe those sobbing gasps –
I will be all right tonight.

Do not wake me later
from my escape into dreams,
let me drift from cloud to cloud
and stumble home.

I am in an OK state of mind.
I am OK,
for now.

The Stillness Of My Fight

What is it
and why do I weep?
I am looking to somewhere for answers
but all I receive is silence,
the dreaded silence.

So I look inside myself,
nothing stirs –
why won't someone answer me?

But if I am still
I hear a faint murmur
whispering my name –
ever so silently I am called;
yet it grows faint again
and I struggle to hear a sound.
All is still
but I know it is there.

Vital Awakening

I have never felt this way before,

a new sensation

parallels a new understanding –

I am free.

I have never felt so much power,

so much excitement –

how does one control it?

When I feel like this

nothing can stop me.

The Lie I Do Not Tell

Filling the empty holes in my heart

with pound upon pound of distraction,

numbing the bittersweet loneliness

of the life I insist on creating.

A movie star walk,

a sophisticated talk,

anything to be someone else;

my fantasy world is a wonderful place

full of adventures and sunshine so bright,

but under the lightness broods ill-smelling odour

so vile it can't be let free.

The mask painted on my face

is the smile I seem to bear,

creating anew some acceptable façade

to face this dissonant world;

but the paint is chipping,

my face distorting –

who am I now?

Resigned

I am sinking,
slowly.
This quicksand feels smooth against my soul
as I descend deeper;
I do not bother to remove myself
or struggle –
too lazy to oppose
and too exhausted to care –
I would rather slowly sink into my oblivion
than attempt this futile fight.
I am a hopeless, sad girl
awaiting the last grain of sand
to muffle my silent screams.

Even My Skin Feels Foreign

Is he looking at me,

is she staring at me,

why does everyone scrutinize?

I shift and try to slowly breathe

but realize they notice my discomfort –

what will they think,

how should I act,

why does it even matter?

Niceness

There is niceness oozing from my pores,
seeping back into my skin
to make me believe
that it is all that I am supposed to consist of.
Every muscle,
every bone
is made from niceness,
which continually dies and is reborn again.

But that is not all that I am.
I see it go down the shower drain
only to be born again;
I soak in it while in the bath
where it always appears reborn;
I step into the rain
and it feels so good to be cleansed
deeply into my soul,
but it is always born again.

New

So this is me.
Both eyes wide open,
seeing as if for the first time;
no pretence,
nothing to hide behind –
I am left with only myself.

My beauty has never looked so pure,
so fascinating,
so rich;
there is no barrier between me and the world
to hide behind;
I have cleaned up,
eliminated excess,
left lighter,
freer
and, somehow,
fuller.

Waging War

I am brutal,

playing every part of the army;

I attack

the innocent opponent

and show no sign of relenting.

I cannot let up.

I have won,

yet I cannot stop myself from destroying it all;

compulsion takes control of me

and only I can stop it –

I am Hitler in disguise,

trying to kill my imperfections.

The Cause Of All

Guilt fills my bones,

causing my skin to stretch

into unwanted fat

that covers my soul;

I need to purify

what inhabits my body,

physically remove

the built-up residue

that chokes my whispering voice –

so much disorder and chaos inside,

can you see it filling this room,

these streets,

the world?

Unwelcome Girl

Take off my mask

to reveal the truth –

what happens when

I cannot allow what is beneath?

The vulnerable little girl

I said I would never be –

it is her,

she is me.

My Angel

I call you, sweetheart,
into my opened soul;
I feel your light filling me,
my every bone;
I feel your presence touch me
as a tear steps down my cheek;
I feel you engulf me
into the safety that I need.

Your song is like the sweetness
of honey from a bee,
your touch a guiding hand
taking me back home,
your heart beats like the rhythm
of an ancient drummer's drum,
your presence like an endless candle
flickering inside my soul.

I call you, sweetheart,
into my opened soul;
take my hand and guide me
into the light, the dark, to me;

gently pull me when I falter
and push me when I pause,
take me to my inner self,
my angel, where I belong.

This Body

I am sorry for all the pain I have caused,
for all those knives
I have stabbed you with.

I am sorry for all the times I have beaten you up,
for every time I have bruised you
and made you sick.

I am sorry for hating you without reason,
for hiding you,
for flaunting you,
for making you feel worthless –
I feel worthless.

I am trying
so hard
to treat you well,
but I just cannot seem to
get it right.

Yet you stand by me everyday,
giving me life and supporting me,

never judging,

and even after all the wounds I have inflicted

you are still always there for me.

Please forgive me.

Bleak Outlook

At 4:00 in the morning –
oblivious to myself,
blind to all around me –
I shuffle through my empty space
void of all life.

At 4:00 in the morning –
aware of my heavy body,
scanning the mess I have made –
I fall onto my bed with a thud,
void of all life.

I am void of all life.

Scraping

His silence etches my delicate bones,
tearing
until I cry out in pain,
ripping through my skin,
bleeding and sore,
finally open for those who look close enough.

His silence etches my delicate bones,
screaming its way into my muted heart.

Pieces Of Me

Revolving consumers

in my everlasting parlour,

waiting apprehensively

to pounce on my depleted energy;

hungry,

longing,

licking their lips

in anticipation of my flesh.

But still I hear my yearning heart

tempered by light of day,

hurtling all that hurts

into a bottled jar inside of me –

the echoes of this night

will engulf the lonely-coated stars.

A Child

I sit cross-legged here
soaking up your brilliance,
your light beckoning me to greater heights –
I am enraptured by the wisdom
you impart.

Youth are on the streets outside
looking for me;
but as I sit here,
an ancient newborn,
I know they will never find me.

Expansion

Fire burning instantaneously

as I open up to the sky –

head flung back,

eyes closed,

embracing the turmoil

that tears me apart.

Stillness,

except for the erupting flames of passion

rioting to be freed.

The Struggle

Confusion.
Emotions trapped inside of my stomach
contending to be let out
but not knowing where to go.

Extreme.
Manic ups and downs
that pull me as I struggle,
trying to take over
and wrench me apart.

But it is just me I am fighting,
grappling onto my sanity
before I am washed away
in my own tears.

An Image Of Myself

Do not try to befriend me

I will not be there for you;

do not try to trust me

I will deceive you;

do not try to take me to bed

I will torture you;

do not try to help me out

I will scar you;

do not even care for me

I will toss you out;

and most of all

do not try to love me –

I will break your heart into pieces.

Safety Net

How do I know if it is you
to let my guard down with,
to abandon my thoughts
and surrender?
Can I say your name
in the whispers of a child
and open myself to you?

Just realize it is a game that I play
to avoid potential pain;
and like a chameleon
into myself I change
and wait for your repulsion to come.

But please do not mistake
the sacrifice you have made,
I will only be here for awhile;
just tell your friends
it is a game of pretend
and you will return by the next full moon.

If you are tired of seeing me

or failing to hear me,

remember it is only my game –

lost in the dark

afraid of the light,

I cower behind my veil.

Suspect

Intruder into my sealed cavern
without knowledge of
more than my name –
you are all I ever needed,
the one I wanted least –
are you even concerned with
the world's mastery of tearing me apart,
or are you just another
cheap spectator?

Unseen Path

I am fighting,
physically pulling myself away
from devouring my shame;
I have only given myself the choice
of the familiar road with cut up terrain
or the other,
with perfectly tended gardens –
I cannot let myself give up now.
This magnetic pull
seems stronger than humanly possible to resist,
but I fight.

My feet unsteadily plant themselves
on a hidden cobbled path
of both beauty and shadows,
roses and thorns –
that is good enough for now.

Stay Away

I hate myself
now,
it is too putrid
inside of me for words;
a vile smell
and hideous image
run through my veins,
seething to be rescued –
it is trapped inside of me,
too cowardly to escape.

Running From A Cruel World

As light as a feather

as high as the clouds

over and over

I drop,

down to the earth

where I cannot stay,

which pushes me with all of its power

until I run away

again,

into the dark labyrinth

of this bottomless pit

where I wait for

sunshine to break through.

Our Moment Together

We sit as two best friends
enjoying our memories and laughter,
reminiscing about old times
and smiling at our worst.

But then I realize
how little you know me;
my other life has been so well-guarded
that even you do not know where I have been.

And it is strange to think
of how we are both living this same moment
but feeling so completely different;
my mind distorts our laughter
into self-conscious faking –
how do you not see through me?

Voracious

I am grasping at stale air,
pleading for that something
to fill me up:
lost
hopeless
wandering in oblivion,
desperate for an answer.
I search for solid ground
where I will stumble but do not fall
upon rocks
awaiting my arrival;
so I anxiously pause
and wait
for a warm burst of air
to guide me in a healthy direction.

The Layers I Etch

The fears I carve,

the pain I scrape,

in tormenting cycles

I yield;

seeking relief

of this ceaseless sadness,

so weary and familiar:

I say farewell to silent cries

screaming to be heard;

I bid adieu to heavy nights

of regret and solitude;

I am finished with bowing my head,

smiling,

and pretending all is fine.

Bad

I see you
and I want to be you;
jealousy rises in my cloudy mind
and I hate you
for your waste-less body.

You stay with me all day,
all night;
all I feel is anxiety
at your barren flesh,
wondering how to dispose of my own.
No matter how hard I push you away,
try to believe you are bad,
I seek your perfection –
intriguing,
so remarkable I stare,
and yearn…

Balancing Myself

This insatiable urge

inside of me

forces my breath to hemorrhage;

I will it to compose itself,

hoping it will hear;

everyday I walk on

this thin tightrope –

I have fallen so many times

it now feels better down here.

For You

Why is it so hard

to see a frown upon my face,

a tear glisten on my cheek,

pain in my eyes so deep –

do you think it hurts you more than me?

You could not feel this pain as I do;

depression sinks so deeply in my skin,

my bones,

my self.

I have stabbed my heart,

slashed my soul,

burned right through my veins;

but I conceal this struggle

to keep a pretty smile upon my face,

for you.

Shimmer

Glistening beauty running down a cheek,
an outpouring of sensitive emotion –
nothing more expressive
than the eye from which the tear was born.

I Turn Away

Mistrust of people
who are not myself,
separated by my defensive wall of stone;
I peak around the corner
and see nothing but
bitter emptiness;
somehow my empty void
fills you up
but only leaves me lonely –
I struggle to turn and face you
but end cowering where I cannot be seen.

My Gift

I have a gift.
It came in a box
wrapped with spikes and poison;
one look at it,
years later,
and I am repulsed –
the asshole critics
sitting in their comfy chairs,
the fires in the pit of
some dark purgatory
somewhat resembling a stomach –
all adorned the paper.

So why did I open
this filthy and disgusting box?
I hope one day to figure that out.

Suppressed Fury

The murmur of my silence

etches slashes in my soul,

penetrating my demeanour

as a little girl;

deeper,

burning embers

embed themselves in my skin,

the only proof of my destruction,

trapped in the suppressed stillness

of resonant fury.

Superficial Admiration

Sunken skin

hanging on swollen bones

fighting to stay attached –

give me one reason to be beautiful.

Glazed eyes

with a poisonous tongue,

daring you to mess with me;

'cause I won't smile today

and I won't go your way –

I am sick of my shallow attempt

for admiration.

So give me one,

just one,

reason to be beautiful.

I Have Already Started Running

At first

a light began to flicker,

catching my wavering eyes;

I felt it growing into

a blaze of flames,

igniting the spark that woke me.

I have comfort in the uncertainty

I will never be with you –

you who makes my body tremble

and senses scream –

comfort in knowing you will leave;

but still I wait,

my life flashing by

as I blink to comprehend

your absence.

My Concealed Monster

Undulating waves

crash over my still body

trying to cleanse through my pores,

washing away the carrion

and replacing it with sadness;

I am consumed with heavy dread,

not knowing what it looks like

but feeling it tug firmly at my arm –

I despair at the thought

of my soul being hideous.

The Hopeful Mirage

Do I detect a ray of light?
I can feel its warmth
I can taste its sweetness
I can hear its song
I can almost touch its rays;
I smell its warm embrace
and see it, almost within my grasp.

But is it really there?
I am scared to walk towards it
for fear of finding more darkness,
but if it is there
I cannot let it fade –
I need this small ray of light
to brighten up my sombre cave.

I tremble as I step forward
but take that first stride,
the cold ground shifts
as I steady myself;
while I make my way towards life
doubts creep up in my mind,

but this light inside of me

cannot be let go of

until it is mine.

Suffocating

Thick, odorous,

blackened smoke

presses down on my body,

forcing me to gasp –

why does no one feel it but me?

I am smothered in poisons

I cannot set free;

you try to save me

but only encourage

this overcast haze.

Please

I shriek in pain –
stop it!
But I can't.
I cannot stop the deafening cries
that wake me from my sleep,
that torture me everyday,
that yell at me in silence.
I am scared,
scared to fight it
and scared to lose.

I cannot be strong;
I wish it were all over,
a faint memory –
I cannot imagine ever being free.

The Answer

I need to know
but I cannot find out,
I want the knowledge
but my mind blanks out.

I grasp intellectually with all of my might
but cannot hold on;
I fight, I struggle,
but I never win.

The hunger overbears me
and I need to know now,
but I just, damn it, I cannot grasp it;
it slips through my clawed brain
and laughs at my ignorance,
only to make me want it more.

Still More

Slowly as layers
shed from my bulky shadow
trying to expose the light,
I see a glimmer in the distance
flashing in front of me
and lingering momentarily –
but will this stop
the elusive battle
to dispose of my sins,
or is there ever-more
awaiting my fortitude
and tears?

This One Suits Me

It is amazing,
this thing called life;
how can I express
this fountain of energy
that wells up inside of me,
threatening to expose itself
through my skin.
How do I deal with
this incomprehensible well of emotions
I never knew I possessed?
Where did they all come from
and where will they go?

This trip I am on
has revealed to me myself,
and what a strange face has emerged;
one I have seen before,
fleetingly,
that has disappeared beneath
resistance and fear,
replaced by a store-bought mask.

A High Price

A golden heart is broken
by another tortured soul
for the glory of acceptance;
listen and you will hear
the cry of pain,
so faint,
so obvious,
covered with discipline and control,
buried beneath young, blank faces.

Just Smile

I am dying inside.
There is a gnawing pain,
a hunger so submerged
that it will never satiate;
it eats away at me
until there is nothing left
but a body gliding through life.
You want recognition?
Let it eat and eat,
emptying you out.
Put on a smile.
Now watch them flock.

Elusive Obstacle

It is hard to remember when my heart was free
and my soul swayed with the music,
floating up and down the hills of grass
watching the scenes unfold.

I became stuck.
I kept digging deeper and deeper
into the same hole,
engulfing myself to negate all feeling;
for so long I ignored the heavy rocks
plunging down on my soul,
or the light fading to my freedom.

Now that these rocks are being uncovered
and I am bathed in the light I had forgotten,
I cannot seem to walk away from this deep hole
I have nursed for so long,
luring me, repulsing me,
abusing me, saving me,
but always a part of me.

An Image Of You

My hand slowly releases,

carefully,

each finger revealing

your potent image.

Trembling,

it opens to let you go;

as your flesh begins to wilt

and fade away,

it leaves behind a scent –

I'm not sure if I like it –

as each finger recoils

into my empty relief,

my indecisive hand

anticipates its reopening,

carefully watching my heart.

The Same

Your world is so different from mine.
The hurt, pain and stabbing of your heart
is external;
the world looks dim
because you know the darkness on the streets.

My world is so different from yours.
The hurt, pain and stabbing of my heart
is internal;
the world looks dim
through the vacuum of my eyes.

Yet this is the very same world.
Coming from such opposite beginnings,
we are ultimately the same;
I understand your pain in such a way
that it becomes my own –
because the battle is the same
we can fight together.

Gone

Do I want to live,

can I keep going through each day in this haze?

I really do not know how much more I can take.

I am sick of being sick,

tired of feeling like shit,

exhausted from all this time spent

fighting myself.

But I cannot stop it,

it will not let me go

and I hold onto it tightly –

what is it

that I fear so much?

Craving.
Self-destructing.
Purging.
Crying.
Gone.

Meantime

Disorder reigns

as my mind tries to filter

the demon's chatter in my head –

it is so hard to live without it,

that which has taught me,

exhibited me

and left me all alone –

can I fill the appalling void it encompasses

and look myself in the eyes?

Where does it come from,

when will it stop

and what do I do in the meantime?

Dependable

Craziness

in my heart fills me up:

where I sense a void

where I see a hole

where I cannot look

where I dare to see

where I hate myself

where I shine so bright

and where I try to hide –

I hold onto my

craziness

for comfort.

Polluted Self

A dark, smoky cloud
expels itself from me,
engulfing my body
and strangling my blackened breath;
filth gushes through my veins,
pumping my heart with
contaminated fluid –
I gasp despairingly
for any scent
of nourishing oxygen
but find only muddied tears
which spill from my puffy eyes,
fighting to be freed
from my poisonous grip.

I Felt Fine

I was exposed.

I sat in front of strangers

and let them see

the womb of my emotions,

giving them a glimpse

of the truest form of myself;

I showed these people

my most safely guarded secret –

pain.

I showed them,

if only for a second,

my most feared weakness,

yet by doing this

it became my strength;

sitting still

I let them wrap their arms

around my naked soul.

I felt fine.

The Unlocked Cell

Utter disgust
seeps into my mouth
as I live in my bare prison cell –
no bars, no windows,
just cold, cement walls;
I am forever trudging through my maze
as hunter and then hunted,
trying to contain myself
in this horrible skin of mine;
I climb without a ladder,
I fall without wings –
what a horrible crash.

Help

Somebody take me away,

I do not want to live this way anymore;

I am wasted, used up

and cannot catch my breath –

someone save me from

this awful mess

that wretches up my soul.

Hear Me

What would you say if I told you I loved you?
But I would rather announce
your accomplishments,
praise how others regard you,
tell you that no one can replace you,
before I would ever let you know
how I truly feel.
It is that simple –
I cannot let you know me.

(I do love you)

What I Cannot Find

With myself I am not satisfied;
behind this façade of happiness
lies blind terror and darkness,
my essence lost behind a mask
of frivolous glances –
what do I long for?
Always something
that is not anything
and I cannot hide from it forever.

The inner torment
stirs my hollow soul,
tearing away all reason.

Solid Ground

Today was the greatest day of my life –
not because of what the scales said,
not because I ate perfectly
and not because I looked flawless.

But because I lived.
I let myself enjoy the moments
and it felt good.

Today I lived without an eating disorder
and I do not want to ever go back.

Cycle Of Destruction

I am back.

I keep tumbling through,

on and on,

looking inside of myself

to find something,

anything to hold onto;

the cycle rebirth's

and I am born again

into my world of torment

and utter despair.

I am back.

My World

I am stuck in a world of inferiority
where so many sufferers dwell,
it is far removed from everyday life
that to some it does not exist.

It is a place where I trust
all the phonies and fakes
and let them take pieces of me;
it is a sad place, not far away,
where I do not trust a soul with my feelings.
I do not have to if I live this way.

I feel so small –
I cannot reach the depths of sickness,
the arms of poverty,
the knuckles of racism –
my world is so secluded
that nothing else exists but me.

I am so absorbed in my own dramas
that nothing else matters but me.

The Extent of My Love

I wonder at your probing eyes

as your music fills my ears –

do you think you can reach me?

This seamless repetition

of such beautiful notes

catches my heart

as I push you away –

my timid and foreboding mind

outweighs the carnal urge

I feel for you.

No Space For Me

I am living inside of a box
that was made for me long ago;
but everyday I struggle to move
and everyday it gets harder to breathe.

Each moment I grow in space
and realize this box is too small;
it is used up and worn out
and I have not even begun to flourish.

If only I could break down the walls
and take up more space,
jump in the air and scream aloud –
but I do not want to use up too much air
or get in someone's way;
so I will try to be content in my little box,
smiling and staying small.

An Amazing Machine

My car has been broken down
for quite some time –
it still runs when it needs to but is wearing thin.

Lately I have noticed a change.
Someone told me that it did not
have to run this way,
that it could run much smoother;
so I started by gently giving it gas
and changing the oil
and waited to see what would happen –
it stopped stalling!
I could tell that my car
just needed a little bit of care.

So I cleaned it;
it does not look brand new,
but I am starting to see a shine.

I am going to start dealing with
the brakes, the starter,
the engine and the transmission –

it will be a long process

but ultimately rewarding;

I will make sure to

spend the time it takes to make it mine.

I can already see its beauty peaking through.

F-A-T

Why do I all of a sudden feel so fat?
Fat when I touch my skin,
fat when I move a limb –
no bone, no muscle,
just fat;
it covers my body
like a blanket of heavy dread
that I cannot see through –
no skeleton,
even my bones seem to be made of fat;
I want to suck it all away
and become transparent,
but my fat drapes
like a wet sweater on a hanger
and I cannot look in the mirror.

Wicked

As pop culture engulfs
the world in its thin grasp,
shattering innocent victims
one by one,
I cannot help but be entranced.

The flashy clothes
and dazzling smiles,
another disguising lens.

Surrounded by perfection
so easy to attain –
just do not look in the mirror.

Hey, You Are Worthless

I am overcoming you.
You are starving to death
and shrivelling from malnutrition
while I begin to thrive;
I am petrified of disobeying you
but realize you are nothing,
a distortion
that thought it could bully me.
You thought you could hold me down
but instead have taught me:
I am learning confidence despite you,
and I am learning to live because of you,
to love.
With all of your deceit and games,
I am starting to see that you are only that –
tricks and treachery –
who the hell do you think you are
to try and subdue me?

I Can Never Forget

This unbearable pain,
all things inside convulsing,
continually trying to rip me apart;
clenched teeth,
nails embedded –
I seem to forget how badly it hurts –
I refresh my memory as,
wound by wound,
I recall how dark it feels
to be alone
in this self-made purgatory.

Breaking Free

I stand up to speak my voice
leaving Bulimia in my chair;
as I slowly walk towards freedom
I realize how much stronger I am without it;
and as my meek voice speaks louder
I can tell that people understand.

I hear clapping,
applauding of my courage;
as I return to my seat
I proudly sit right on top
of Bulimia
and smile.

Substance

Wallowing in oblivion,
not sure where
the exit is –
hate the heat,
the flames
the scorching of my heart –
I wander aimlessly
through all that matters
and all that does not,
reaching for a semblance
of something meaningful.

Counterfeit Friend

I will not accept this feeling of isolation –
you cannot tell me that I am not good enough,
I am.
No matter how many times
you rear your ugly head,
I will stomp it down twice as hard –
you are not taking control of my life again –
no one but me will make my decisions;
you cannot keep me down any longer
because I will spit on you
and throw things at you,
with all of the power I have;
you will not live inside of me anymore –
I am revealing you to the world
so other innocent victims
will know what you are about.

Do not think I won't.

Assault On My Body

So exhausted from beating you down
tirelessly
for crimes you never committed,
tired of kicking you when
you are on the ground
and powerless,
weary of whipping you raw
and watching you bleed
as you lie trembling on the ground.
But I keep doing it –
why does starvation
keep entering my mind
as the solution to all that is
wrong in the world,
disguising all the horror
with a smile?

Your Bullshit

Now that I realize I am angry
you tell me I want ice cream;
when I feel alienated from people
and frustrated with the world,
ice cream, you say, will soothe me;
well, I do not want ice cream;
I want to yell and scream
and throw a tantrum;
I want to feel enraged,
pure fury,
because I have never felt it before;
it has been stuffed down
and purged out so many times
I have forgotten how to *feel* –
but I feel it now
and it is refreshing.

So, no, I do not want ice cream.
I am pissed off
and I like it.

The Truth I Cannot Bear

What do you think of me now
that I have told you my secret –
am I still the bright girl you love,
or do you see right through me?

I do not deserve all of your love
which might now be repulsion;
I just feel gross
and afraid you will leave
my life forever
because I told the truth.

If you left me I would crumble,
falling to my knees –
your importance in my life
is inexpressible –
but please do not feel pressure to stay
or pressure to love me.

This fight has left me exhausted
and underpaid.
I wish I could quit.

Me

I am moved beyond my thoughts
and tremble in their wake,
rivers run through my blood
without time or place,
sweet sorrow builds my bones
to keep my head held high,
the moisture from my breath
escapes my whetted lips –
I am glistening.
Bitterness drained,
beauty fills my fragile soul;
the insidious voice is as silent as my thoughts
which sleep inside my mind;
my receptive fingers run over the page
gathering strength to continue,
I look deep within my heart,
which yearns to feel my stroke;
I am lifted high above
where my soul connects my body
into one ripened being.
Me.

Destruction Of Destruction

It devours me, a hurt so bad
blood oozes from my clouded heart.

It was you who stabbed me,
you asshole;
you tried to kick me down
but I will not go –
I will stand with my head held high
and fight you until
you lie exuding blackness.
And I will not feel bad.
And I will not help you.
You cannot come into my life
whenever you want
and decide I need a kick –
I will not stand for it.
You have taken from me
too many sleepless nights
and too many lifeless days –
no more;
and even as I cry when I say this,
I mean it –
I am through with you

and I am through with your deceiving games –

I will not play them anymore.

Never again will you taste

the sweetness of my defeat,

my nourishment will go

straight to my hungry heart,

no pit stops along the way.

And I do not care if you make me feel bad,

and I do not care if you scream and shout –

you are worthless

and I do not accept defeat any longer.

You are the one who has made me stronger –

because of you I have found the strength to fight,

and because of you I will fight.

My saviour,

my vilest enemy,

this time I will not give in,

not for the most perfect body in the world.

The World On My Shoulders

War, death, suffering,

I know them all too well;

I live in a poverty of the soul,

I fight in a war with my body,

I die again and again.

I want to hold my arms around the world

and comfort every desperate soul,

but I cannot seem to leave my own mind.

It is so hard to smile

while people are dying –

why can't I save the world?

Clear Light

A ray of light shines through my soul,

lifting my tired body;

no more despair

or self-induced pain,

no more retreating from the world –

you teach me how life is supposed to feel.

As I slowly re-focus my eyes

I see a clear view;

things appear I have long since forgotten,

objects emerge I have never noticed;

the lines are clearer

and I can see what is in front of me –

it all looks so different.

You have helped me to see the world

and how it can be,

thank you for shining your light

to re-kindle mine.

Pushing Away What Matters Most

What I would give to feel
your warmth around me,
the breeze of your voice,
the breadth of your arms;
to feel you here beside me
looking deep into my soul,
seeing who I am.

But before you even glance,
before we ever touch,
I am gone.
I have pulled away
before we could even come together.

And now I am lonely.

Goodnight

As I lay myself down to sleep,
my blankets breathe a breath of ease
and I settle into my hollow.

As every limb is taken by slumber,
my body imprints itself into the mattress
and my thoughts turn to dreams.

I drift into the unconscious world,
my body moves to its own rhythm
and I rock gently back and forth.

Delving deeper into my abyss,
my senses are altered to fantasy
and reality slips away.

As my mind enters into stillness,
my emotions are filtered through my reel
and I am gone for tonight.
Goodnight.

She
(Part two)

It regains its hold,
stronger and stronger
as each day progresses,
as the girl sells herself
to what she does not know –
an evil presence fills her otherwise perfect world,
created for her protection.
As the grip grows steadier
her soul becomes weaker,
beckoning more and more
as it takes over;
piece by piece
her whole self transforms
into what she thinks can never leave her.
Yet she blames herself,
that she deserves to feel this way,
was put on this earth to suffer greatly;
never a thought of self-worth or confidence
that maybe one day she can rid her afflicted body
of this monster
and live a life of happiness.

It has her so whipped by now

that it can manipulate her

to do whatever it pleases,

telling her that it is what she has always wanted,

keeping her locked up in its chamber

waiting,

praying

for a chance of release.

It returns day after day

to make her

feel worthless and fat,

circling until she finally collapses.

This vicious cycle is pushed so far down

but consumes her every thought,

move,

impulse,

taking up every minute of her busy life

without a moment gone by

not thinking of how unworthy she is.

In the grasps of its deadly claws,

she surrrenders to a power unknown,

a power that will one day save her life.

Eating Disorder Resources

National Eating Disorder Information Centre
www.nedic.ca
A Canadian non-profit organization founded in 1985 to provide information and resources on eating disorders. One of their main goals is to inform the public about eating disorders and related issues.

National Association of Anorexia Nervosa and Associated Disorders (ANAD)
www.anad.org
An American non-profit that seeks to prevent and alleviate the problems of eating disorders. ANAD advocates for the development of healthy attitudes, bodies, and behaviours through supporting, educating, and connecting individuals, families and professionals.

National Eating Disorders Association (NEDA)
www.nationaleatingdisorders.org
A non-profit in the US advocating on behalf of and supporting individuals and families affected by eating disorders. Reaching millions every year, they campaign for prevention, improved access to quality treatment, and increased research funding to better understand and treat eating disorders.

beat
www.b-eat.co.uk
Beat is the UK's only nationwide organisation supporting people affected by eating disorders, their family members and friends, and campaigning on their behalf.

EDReferral.com
www.edreferral.com
Since 1999, EDReferral.com has been dedicated to the prevention and treatment of eating disorders.

About the Author

Lori Henry struggled with bulimia and disordered eating for over six years when she was a teenager. She chronicles her experience from sickness to recovery in her book, *Silent Screams: Into and Out Of Bulimia through Poetry* (firsty published in 2002).

Now fully recovered, Lori works as an eating disorder therapist (registered occupational therapist, psychotherapist) in private practice, as well as writes about mental health in publications all over the world.

Lori's website:
www.eatingdisordertherapist.ca

Connect with Lori on social media:
X: @LoriHenry
Facebook: www.facebook.com/LoriHenryTherapy
Bluesky: https://bsky.app/profile/lorihenry.bsky.social
YouTube: @EatingDisorderTherapist

www.ingramcontent.com/pod-product-compliance
Lightning Source LLC
Chambersburg PA
CBHW032041290426
44110CB00012B/904